DAD JOKES

The Best Dad Jokes, Awfully Bad but Funny Jokes and Puns Volume 2

Matthew Cooper

© Copyright 2018 - All rights reserved.

It is not legal to reproduce, duplicate, or transmit any part of this document in either electronic means or in printed format. Recording of this publication is strictly prohibited.

Table Of Contents

DAD JOKES 1

Table Of Contents 3

FREE AUDIOBOOK 4

Introduction 5

Chapter 1: Fruit and Veggie Jokes 7

Chapter 2: Light Bulb 26

Chapter 3: Iowans 34

Chapter 4: Yo Mama.. 38

Chapter 5: Knock Knock... for Kids 44

Chapter 6: Christmas Jokes 54

Chapter 7: Weather Jokes.. 68

Chapter 8: Valentine 76

Chapter 9: Thanksgiving.. 84

Chapter 10: Birthday! 92

Chapter 11: Coffee 101

Chapter 12: General Wordplay............................... 110

Chapter 13: Creative Answering Machine Messages 140

Thank You! 145

Don't Forget! 147

FREE AUDIOBOOK

Don't have an Audible Account and would like to listen to the audio version for FREE?

Click the link below and sign up; to receive **"Dad Jokes: The Best Dad Jokes, Awfully Bad but Funny Jokes and Puns Volume 2"** Audiobook for Free!

For US: http://bit.ly/DadJokes2

For UK: http://bit.ly/DadJokes2UK

Introduction

Hello!

Thanks for purchasing *"Dad Jokes: The Best Dad Jokes, Awfully Bad but Funny Jokes and Puns Volume 2!"*

Sometimes nothing makes more sense than a good, old-fashioned corny joke to make the heart merry, and put a smile on everyone's face. Dad jokes or bad jokes, either one is fine. They sometimes do the trick.

Perhaps you've already joined me in *"Dad Jokes: The Best Dad Jokes, Awfully Bad but Funny Jokes and Puns"*. The first hilarious book to the series. If not, don't worry, you'll find this volume just as painfully funny. I intend to take it a step better in this volume.

There's something in here about Fruits and Vegetables, Light Bulbs, Christmas, Weather, Valentine, Thanksgiving, and Birthdays. Oh, Iowans, Coffee Lovers, Kids, and Mothers have got my love in here. Then, if you subject answering phone calls to answering machines, you will love the last chapter; it was dedicated to you.

People always say the secret to a good book is to start with something of specific interest to the reader. I wish I could tell you, "See Chapter 2, Number 6 for a free ticket to a trip round the world." But I'll start with a story. I hope you enjoy the disclaimer that comes after the story, and the jokes that come after the disclaimer… you could still see Chapter 2 Number 6 for your ticket, though.

Certain American tourists applied to go for a guided adventure across the Sahara Desert. When they arrived at the starting point, they were shocked to find out that a camel was going to be their ride through the entire journey.

They expressed their disgust to the expedition leader, who took time to make them understand that no vehicle made could survive the route they're taking across the desert.

"This trip can only be made by specially prepared camels," Omar said.

One of the Americans asked, "How special can the preparations be?"

Omar replied, "Um, first the camel takes water but as he's about getting filled with his last sip, I'll slam these two bricks on his nuts for the camel to suck up another ten gallons of water sufficient to carry him through the long journey."

"Won't that hurt?" asked the American.

Omar replied, "Only if I catch my fingers between the bricks."

I think I shouldn't bore with stories that I don't exactly like saying. I'll prefer we go the jokes way, as that is what the journey you're about to embark on is about.

You can find your way through this journey by opening each page the way a navigator uses stars, but you have to be extremely careful, so you don't miss your way into laughs, rib cracks, and getting torn apart. So, save gas for every kilometer you go.

Chapter 1: Fruit and Veggie Jokes

As a fruit lover, I'm sort of partial to jokes of the fruit variety. Some of them are so corny they embarrass me, some make me cringe a little, while some are just extremely funny. The best thing about them is that they're fruity and have zero calories, just the best for a vegetarian.

It's an amazing moment to treat yourself and get equipped with some family-friendly and admittedly corny jokes, that can bring some humor and levity to your family timeout, and fill everyone with juicy laughter.

Here are my favorite clean and washed vegetable jokes.

1

What do we call a vampire's best fruit?

A neck-tarine!

2

How do ghosts eat apples?

By goblin them!

3

What do you call a ghost's best fruit?

Boo-berries.

4

When do you call an apple a grouch?

When it's a crab apple!

5

What do you call apples that play trumpets?

A tooty fruity!

6

What did the skin of the apple say to it?

I've got you covered.

7

Why did the apple and orange remain single?

Because the banana split.

8

What food does King Kong love most?

Ape-ricots!

9

When two bananas meet each other, only one thing is involved

A banana shake!

10

Banana peels are used to make a special kind of shoe…

Slippers!

11

For what reason did the banana go see the doctor?

It wasn't peeling well.

12

There were two bananas in the sun, do you know what one said to the other?

I'm not sure about you, but I'm starting to peel!

13

What kind of key opens a banana?

A monkey.

14

What's a tailor's favorite kind of vegetable?

A string bean!

15

What kind of vegetable is jealous?

A green bean.

16

The people danced to the vegetable band, why?

It had a good beet.

17

What is green and goes to a summer camp?

A Brussels' scout.

18

What's the strongest vegetable?

A muscle sprout.

19

Why do cabbages win races?

They are better at getting a-head!

20

How did the farmer fix his jeans?

With a cabbage patch!

21

What kind of vegetable will you find a taxi driver eats more of?

A Cab-bage!

22

What did the Mama melon say to the baby melon's boyfriend?

You Can't-Eloupe.

23

What type of flower should not be kept in a vase?

Cauliflower.

24

What did the first carrot hear the other carrot say?

Is it just me or is it actually orange in here?

What was the second carrot's response?

Hold on a minute, I have to root around for the answer!

25

What type of vegetable is found specifically in the basement?

Cellar-ee!

26

What is brown, hairy, and wears sunglasses?

A coconut on vacation.

27

What is an ear of corn?

It is the kind of vegetable most likely to be a rock and roll fan.

28

What would you hear an embarrassed corn say?

"Aw, shucks!"

29

Why is it unwise to tell secrets in a cornfield?

Because there are too many ears!

30

Why will a corn stalk get mad at the farmer?

Because the farmer keeps pulling its ears!

31

What does Cornelius call his silly friends?

Corn flakes!

32

When does corn get cob webs?

When it's left it in the barn for too long.

33

What did the little cob of corn call his dad?

Pop Corn!

34

What is corn that joins the army called?

Kernel

35

What's the one thing an ear of corn is better at?

It's the vegetable with the best hearing in the field.

36

How does the rooster wake up Cornelius Corn?

Cob-a-doodle-do!

37

Where do cucumbers go for a date?

The salad bar!

38

Why is History the fruitiest school subject?

Because it is full of dates

39

What's an egg-plant?

A chicken's favorite vegetable?

40

What is purple, delicious, and fun to decorate for Easter?

A hard-boiled eggplant!

41

Do you know what happens when you sit on a grape?

It lets out a little wine!

42

Why aren't grapes ever lonely?

Because they come in bunches!

43

Why did the grape stop in the middle of the road?

Because he ran out of juice.

44

What vegetable can't you take on a boat?

Leeks.

45

What is row-maine?

A kayaker's favorite kind of lettuce.

46

What did the hungry kid hear the salad greens say?

We'll make your mouth and tummy happy, only if you lett-uce!

47

What did the lettuce say to the celery?

Stop stalking me!

48

What was the salad's comments to the dressing?

Lettuce be friends!

49

What room can be eaten?

A mushroom!

50

Why do Ms. Mushroom and Mr. Mushroom go out with each other?

Because Mr. Mushroom is a fungi (fun guy)!

51

What is the outcome of crossing a potato with an onion?

A potato with watery eyes!

52

Why was the man at the orange juice factory sacked?

He couldn't concentrate!

53

Have you heard the joke about the peach?

It's pit-iful!

54

What are twins' favorite fruit?

Pears!

55

What do vegetables desire in the world more than anything else?

Peas (peace) on earth!

56

Why do you think vegetables want peas so much on earth?

Because it will give them peas of mind!

57

When two peas fight it results in only one thing?

Black-eyed peas.

58

When is an apple not an apple?

When it's a pineapple!

59

What type of fruit do trees love most

Pine-apple.

60

What is that fruit that fixes sinks?

A PLUM-ber!

61

How do you fix a cracked pumpkin?

With a pumpkin patch!

62

Why are radishes smart?

Because they're so well-red!

63

What's the coolest vegetable?

A rad-ish!

64

What is small, red and whispers?

A hoarse radish!

65

Why were the strawberries so upset?

Because they were in a jam!

66

What is a scarecrow's favorite fruit?

Straw-berries!

67

What's a dancer's favorite kind of vegetable?

Spin-ach!

68

What's the most uncomfortable kind of vegetable?

Spin-ouch!

69

Why was the pumpkin angry at the sweet potato?

Because the sweet potato said, "I yam what I yam"

70

Why did the Tomato go to prom with a prune?

Because he couldn't find a date!

71

How do you fix a broken tomato?

Tomato paste!

72

Why was the tomato blushing?

Because it saw the salad dressing.

73

What did the father tomato say to the baby tomato whilst on a family walk?

Ketchup.

74

What do you call a vegetable addicted to looking at animals?

A zoo-chini!

75

What is a zucchini's favorite game?

Squash!

Chapter 2: Light Bulb

If you're like me who didn't find humor in light bulb jokes till I was 22, I'm about to change that! There are hundreds of them, but I've resolved to resist the impulse of going beyond twenty-five of them.

It is possible to come up with an unlimited number of variations of these jokes by substituting a particular ethnic, social, or racial groups into these jokes. Just so I don't spoil the fun, I didn't pick on a single ethnic group because there is so many worth picking on.

WARNING! This chapter contains contents that may be offensive to the following people:

Irishmen, psychiatrists, Zen masters, feminists, narcissists, women, men, programmers, surgeons, students, executives, teachers, writers, psychologists, Marxists, accountants, and everyone… and by now, every other profession who is offended to have been left off this list.

1

How many Irishmen are needed to change a light bulb?

Fifteen. One to hold the bulb and the other fourteen to drink whiskey till the room starts to spin.

2

How many psychiatrists are needed to change a light bulb?

Two, however the bulb must want to be changed by one of them.

3

How many Zen masters are needed to change a light bulb?

Two. One to change it and the remaining person not to change it.

4

How many feminists are needed to change a light bulb?

Twenty. One to change it and the remaining nineteen to form a support group.

5

How many I.B.M. engineers are needed to change a burnt light bulb?

None. All they do is check the quality of the darkness and get the customers to upgrade.

6

How many narcissists are needed to change a light bulb?

One. He holds the bulb while the world revolves around him.

7

How many women with PMS are needed to change a light bulb?

Six.

Why?

Okay, none. The bulb just changes, okay?

8

How many real men are needed to change a light bulb?

None. Darkness doesn't scare real men.

9

How many advertising execs are needed to change a light bulb?

Hhhhhmmmmm... isn't that an interesting question?

10

How many art students are needed to change a light bulb?

One, but he gets two credits.

11

How many grad students are needed to change a light bulb?

One, but they need ten years to do it.

12

How many programmers are needed to change a light bulb?

None. That's not a software problem, it's hardware.

13

How many surgeons are needed to change a lightbulb?

None. You don't need it out today, but if it continues to give you trouble in the future, you should think of removing it.

14

How many psychanalysts are needed to change a light bulb?

One is enough, but the bulb must want to change, and it can take years.

15

How many college basketball players does it take to change a light bulb?

Everyone on the team! And they all get a semester's credit for it!

16

How many religious education teachers does it take to screw in a light bulb?

One, and their God of choice.

17

How many surrealists are needed to change a lightbulb?

Ten, one to change the lightbulb, and the other nine to wrestle with the giant gecko in the bathroom!

18

How many surrealists are needed to change a lightbulb?

Two. One to hold the giraffe and the other nine to put the clocks in the bathtub.

19

How many boring people are needed to change a lightbulb?

One.

20

How many mystery crime novel writers are needed to change a lightbulb?

Two. One to think of the plot, the other to give it a really good twist.

21

How many balls of wool are needed to change a lightbulb.

One, but it has to be very large.

22

How many punk rockers are needed to change a lightbulb?

Two. One to change the bulb and the other to kick the chair out from underneath him.

23

How many surrealists are needed to change a lightbulb?

One, to get to the other side.

24

How many surrealists are needed to change a lightbulb?

Two. One to do it, and the other to hold the fish.

25

How many surrealists are needed to change a light bulb?

Three. One to hold the giraffe and the other two to fill the bathtub

with brightly colored machine tools.

Chapter 3: Iowans

I decided to write a few jokes about Iowa for three reasons. First, I heard about the skeleton they found in the closet at the Iowa State campus in 2005. They said he was the winner of the 1965 hide and seek contest. He was apparently still hiding.

Secondly, I heard an Iowan died and went to Heaven but was stopped by Saint Peter who said, "Before I let you in, you have to pass a test." "Oh, no!" she replied, but Saint Peter said, "Don't worry, it isn't difficult. Just answer the question - Who was God's Son?" Even I was shocked when my friend told me she thought and finally answered, "Andy!" I guess Saint Peter was shocked too, because he repeated the response, "Andy?" The Iowan said, "Yes, we usually sang it in choir practice and in church: Andy walks with me, Andy talks with me, Andy tells me I am his own."

Finally, in 2016, I was at a hardware store in Iowa, so this Iowan walks into the hardware store to buy a chainsaw. Dude says, "I want one that'll cut down about ten trees in an hour." So, the clerk sold him one. I left not knowing how the story ended, When I went back a week later, I heard the Iowan came in the next day all upset and saying, "Hey, this chainsaw only cut down one small tree per hour!" The clerk told me he replied and said, "Gee, let me take a look at it." And he pulled on the starter rope and the saw started up and the Iowan said, "Hey, what's that noise?"

Okay, just so it doesn't literally begin to sound noisy, let's read about Iowans.

1

How do you make an Iowan's eyes light up?

Flash a light in his ear.

2

Do you know why Iowans don't like making chocolate chip cookies?

Because it takes too long to peel the m&ms.

3

Iowans love to use birth control pills.

Just so they'll remember what day of the week it is.

4

But they stopped using the birth control pills.

Simply because the pills kept falling out.

5

Why do Iowans hate making Jello?

Because they don't know how best to get two cups of water into those little bags.

6

Why don't Iowans eat pickles?

Because they can't get their heads in the jar.

7

It's easy to know if an Iowan has used your computer.

You'll find eraser marks on the screen.

8

What do Iowa cheerleaders do on the field at halftime?

They Graze.

9

What happened to the Iowan who stayed up all night to see where the sun went to?

It finally dawned on him.

10

What happened to the Iowan who went to check out a book called "How to Hug" at the library?

She got home and found out it was volume seven of the encyclopedia.

11

Why don't Iowans take coffee breaks?

It takes too long to retrain them.

Chapter 4: Yo Mama

I know that by now, everyone's heard a "Yo Mama" joke, or even attempted cracking one themselves. After all, they have been popular as far back as the '90s, and thanks to my mama's mama, I came to realize they've actually been around for much longer than that. In fact, "Yo Mama" jokes date all the way back to the classical ages before my mama's mama's mama's mama's mama. I mean, my mama's so young that her age is the last two digits of the number of years the yo mama joke has been around for.

It's one of the funniest joke niches, so funny that a TV show was named after it – Yo Mama Show, and MTV launched Yo Momma TV. One wonders who started it, but then, I also love my mama so much that I could name a TV show after her, just that my mama's so cool she'd feature only as the title of the show.

I wish I could see my mama every day to tell her my book of jokes has a paragraph on her – my mama is so funny she'll probably tell me that she always knew I wouldn't do so much as dedicate the whole page to her. While writing this chapter, I thought about it and told myself I'd prefer to have my mama's mouth on every pages of this chapter spilling the yo mama jokes, but then, my mama isn't made of paper. So, let's get down to read the pages as written by no one else (including my mother) but me.

1

Your mama is so fat,

People think she's backing up when her beeper goes off.

2

Your mama is so fat,

When she goes to see a movie at the cinema, she sits next to everyone.

3

Your mama is so fat,

When she goes in a restaurant, she sees the menu and says, "Okay."

4

Your mama is so fat,

She irons her pants on the driveway.

5

Your mama is so fat,

She applies her lipstick with a paint roller.

6

Your mama is so fat,

She can't get in her pocket without pulling down her pants.

7

Your mama is so fat,

You have to take two buses and a train and two buses to get on her good side.

8

Your mama is so fat,

She has to wake up in sections.

9

Your mama's so fat,

A booger popped out of George Washington's nose when she sat on

a quarter.

10

Your mama is so fat,

She put on some BVD's and they spelled boulevard by the time she got them on.

11

Your mama is so fat,

The National Weather Service has a name for every fart she releases.

12

Your mama is so ugly,

They're going to move Halloween to her birthday.

13

Your mama is so ugly,

She makes onions cry.

14

Your mama is so ugly,

She went to the salon and it took five hours for an estimate.

15

Your mama is so ugly,

Cats try to put sand on her when she goes to the beach.

16

Your mama is so old,

They didn't have history when she was in school.

17

Your mama is so old,

When I told her to act her age, she died.

18

Your mama's so fat,

When she's at the corner and the police drive by, they say "Hey! Break it up!"

Chapter 5: Knock Knock… for Kids

Knock knock! Who's there? Our. Our what… funny jokes, that's who.

I remember when my kids had their holidays, and they had their friends around. They were about to go out to play when the heavy rain started. They almost began swearing and cursing at the rain when a friend of my kids came knocking in the rain, he wanted to join the other bored children in playing. I asked, "Who's that," and that was it. Knock knock jokes for kids began.

The knock knock jokes kept them engrossed for hours together, and got the boredom beaten out of them. And oh, just when I thought they were probably not educative, I realized it kept them thinking and alert in giving swift answers – of course all had puns. They got the hang of it before long and came up with their own jokes. It looked like that was all they did throughout the holidays.

A knock-knock joke is a simple five line "call and response" activity involving two people. It goes like this:

Punster: Knock, knock!

Recipient: Who's there?

Punster: One or two-word response, which could be anything, ranging from a name to a thing, or place, or just anything.

Recipient: Repetition of the reply followed by the word 'who.'

Punster: The punch line, which involves misuse of the word for 'pun.'

Did I just knock on your brain and get you thinking??? Oh yeah, that's the idea. I remember saying in the earlier paragraph that it was probably not educative. Well, that's it, take it however you want.

For anyone who thinks kids are too young to comprehend jokes, think again. Those kids are punsters. Below is a collection of some of the kid-friendly knock-knock jokes told that holiday period.

1

Knock, knock.

Who's there?

Frankfurter.

Frankfurter who?

Frankfurter lovely evening.

2

Knock, knock.

Who's there?

Dexter.

Dexter who?

Dexter halls with boughs of holly.

3

Knock, knock.

Who's there?

Fortification.

Fortification who?

Fortification, we're going to Miami.

4

Knock, knock.

Who's there?

Mr. Walter.

Mr. Walter who?

You don't Mr. Walter until the well runs dry.

5

Knock, knock.

Who's there?

Itzhak.

Itzhak who?

Itzhak sin to tell a lie.

6

Knock, knock.

Who's there?

Earl.

Earl who?

Early bird gets the worm.

7

Knock, knock.

Who's there?

Amos.

Amos who?

Ain't misbehaving,' savin' all my love for you.

8

Knock, knock.

Who's there?

Saul.

Saul who?

Saul there is; there ain't no more.

9

Knock, knock.

Who's there?

Buh.

Buh who?

Don't be sad

10

Knock, knock.

Who's there?

Boo.

Boo who?

Don't cry

11

Knock, knock.

Who's there?

Turnip.

Turnip who?

Turnip the radio please!

12

Knock, knock.

Who's there?

Lettuce.

Lettuce Who?

Lettuce in and you'll find out!

13

Knock, knock.

Who's there?

Bean.

Bean who?

Bean a while since I last saw ya!

14

Knock, knock.

Who's there?

Alison.

Alison who?

Alison Wonderland

15

Knock, knock.

Who's there?

The ever-interrupting cow.

The ever int...

MOOO.

16

Knock, knock.

Who's there?

Canoe.

Canoe who?

Canoe open the door please!

17

Knock, knock.

Who's there?

Dishwasher.

Dishwasher who?

Dish wash er way I spoke till I got my false teeth

18

Knock, knock.

Who's there?

A guy who just had four shots of espresso!

A guy th—

Now repeat after me, "a guy that just had four shots of espresso who?"

19

Knock, Knock.

Who's there?

Frank.

Frank who?

Frank you for being my friend!

20

Knock, Knock.

Who's there?

Emma.

Emma who?

Emma hoping I get a lot of cards on my birthday!

21

Knock, Knock.

Who's there?

Atlas.

Atlas who?

Atlas, it's Valentine's Day!

22

Knock, Knock.

Who's there?

Pooch.

Pooch who?

Pooch your arms around me!

23

Knock, Knock.

Who's there?

Olive.

Olive who?

Olive you!

Chapter 6: Christmas Jokes

Christmas. The season I look forward to. A season of merriment, fun, partying, and prayers. And just as mischievous elves enjoy playing pranks, everyone, especially kids, love to poke fun at Santa. Christmas jokes help break up the monotony and boredom as everyone counts down to the seemingly unending days before Christmas Eve. Also, the stress before the season calls for some shake-inducing laughter like a "bowl full of jelly."

I know what you have in mind, I mean I know your wish right now, and I'll give it to you like you want it. Here are genuinely funny and crazy Christmas season jokes to melt those pre-Christmas holiday stresses away. Add them to your kitty, polish your stand-up comedy act, and be the cynosure of your friends when you next attend a Christmas party. And don't forget to record the smile on the lips of all your friends and loved ones.

Ho-ho-ho with the funny Christmas jokes collection.

1

Why did Scrooge keep a pet lamb?

Because it would say, "Baaaaahh humbug!"

2

What did the salt say to the pepper?

Season's Greetings!

3

Where do you find reindeer?

It depends on where you leave them!

4

Who is a Christmas tree's favorite singer?

Spruce Springsteen.

5

What's Santa's favorite snack food?

Crisp Pringles.

6

Why does Christmas have 25 letters of the alphabet instead of 26?

On Christmas, it has Noel.

7

"Why didn't Rudolph get a good report card?"

"Because he went down in History."

8

What's Elf's Birthday favorite party song?

Freeze A Jolly Good Fellow!

9

What cars do elves drive?

A toy-Yoda.

10

How did Scrooge win the football game?

The ghost of Christmas passed

11

What do you call Santa's helpers?

Subordinate Clauses.

12

What is Santa's primary language?

North Polish.

13

What does a reindeer say before saying a joke?

This will sleigh you

14

Why did the couple get hitched on December 24?

So they could have a married Christmas

15

How do you lift a frozen car?

With a Jack Frost

16

Which holiday mascot has the least spare change?

St. Nickel-less

17

What is an elf who just has won the lottery called?

Welfy

18

How did the ornament get addicted to Christmas?

He was hooked on trees his whole life

19

How do you know a family isn't celebrating Christmas?

The lights are on, but nobody's a gnome.

20

What do you call an obnoxious reindeer?

RUDE-olph.

21

Why do Christmas trees love the future?

Because the presents beneath them.

22

What do you call an elf who sings?

A wrapper!

23

What is a kid who doesn't believe in Santa called?

A rebel without a Claus.

24

What do you call a bankrupt Santa?

Saint Nickel-less.

25

Why should a Christmas tree visit a barber?

Because it needs to be trimmed.

26

What is Santa Claus' laundry detergent of choice?

Yule-Tide.

27

How does Santa keep his bathroom tiles immaculate?

He uses Comet.

28

What's Santa's favorite song by the Ramones?

Blitzen-krieg Bop.

29

Why is The Temptations' version of Silent Night St. Nick's favorite?

Because Santa Was A Rolling Stone.

30

Did you hear that Santa knows karate?

He has a black belt.

31

Who is Santa's favorite singer?

Elf-is Presley.

32

When Father Christmas claps his hands at the end of a play, what do we say he did?

He gave a Santapplause!

33

What would you reply with when Santa takes attendance at school?

Present.

34

Why does Santa have 3 gardens?

So he can ho-ho-ho.

35

Why was Santa's little helper feeling depressed?

Because he had low elf-esteem.

36

What do would you call a Kris Kringle that goes on his wife's health insurance?

A dependent Claus.

37

What is Christmas

The time when everyone gets Santamental.

38

Why did Santa bring 22 reindeer to Walmart?

He brought extra doe incase what he wanted to buy cost more than his planned 20 bucks.

39

What kind of bike does Santa Claus ride?

A Holly Davidson.

40

What is the result of crossing a detective with Father Christmas?

Santa Clues!

41

What do elves call a Santa on the beach?

Sandy Claus

42

Why does Santa go down the chimney?

Because it soots him!

43

What is a Crisp Kringle?

What you get when Santa goes down the chimney when a fire is lit?

44

What did Santa name his dog?

Santa Paws!

45

What's as big as Santa but weighs nothing?

Santa's shadow!

46

Why did Father Christmas put his clock in his sleigh?

He wanted to see time fly!

47

Why does Santa have elves in his workshop?

Because the Seven Dwarves were busy!

48

What did Santa Claus' girlfriend say to him when she looked up to the sky?

Looks like rain, dear!

49

Where does Santa stay when he's on vacation?

At a Ho-ho-ho-tel.

50

How does Santa sing the alphabet?

A B C D E F G …H I J K L M N Oh! Oh! Oh! …P Q R S T U V W X Y Z!

51

How much did Santa pay for his sleigh?

Nothing, it was on the house!

52

What do you call a kid afraid of Santa Claus?

Claustrophobic.

53

Why was Santa given a parking ticket last Christmas Eve?

Because he left his sleigh in a snow parking zone while making a special delivery.

Chapter 7: Weather Jokes

One cold night during autumn, we warmly and comfortably sat in our penthouse listening to the weather report. My sister dreamily asked, "I wonder what the temperature is in Georgia?" My wife added, "I wonder what it is in Iowa!" My grandfather grumpily added, "I wonder what it is in Fahrenheit!"

When we moved north, my family was feeling apprehensive about how severe the winters in our new home would be. In all my anxiety, I decided to ask a native about the weather. She replied, "Sir, we experience only four seasons here, and they are early-winter, late-winter, mid-winter, and next winter."

Sun, rain, or cold weather, anyone will be a cut-up in any climate with the funny weather jokes. While bad weather is snow laughing matter, weather puns sure are. They will trigger a few groans and get your eyes rolling. So, pull everyone out for perfect laughs when the moment strikes, but do not tell these at parties.

1

How does a hurricane see?

With its eye.

2

Can Bees fly in the rain?

Not without their yellow jackets.

3

What is a Queens favorite kind of precipitation?

Reign!

4

What is the Mexican weather report?

Chili today and hot tamale.

5

What did the evaporating raindrop say?

I'm going to pieces.

6

Do you know what the hail storm tell the roof?

This will be no ordinary sprinkles, so hang onto your shingles.

7

What do you call a wet bear?

A drizzly bear

8

What is a two-straight day of rain in Seattle called?

A weekend.

9

What goes up when the rain comes down?

An Umbrella.

10

What does it do before it rains candy?

It sprinkles!

11

Why did the kid use ketchup when it was raining?

Because it rained cats and hot dogs

12

What did one raindrop say to the other?

Two's company, three's a cloud

13

Why does Snoop dog need an umbrella?

Fo' Drizzle.

14

How do you differentiate between the weather and a horse?

One rains down and the other is reined up.

15

When does it rain money?

When there is "change" in the weather.

16

What is a king's favorite kind of precipitation?

Hail!

17

Why did your wife go out with her purse open?

Because she expected some change in the weather.

18

Why will nothing change if global warming continues?

We'll still get a chance to see polar bears in the zoo.

19

What happens when fog lifts in California?

UCLA!

20

What did the first thermometer say to the second one?

You make my temperature rise.

21

What do you call a cow lifted high into the sky by a tornado?

An udder disaster!

22

What did the first lightning bolt say to the second one?

You're shocking!

23

What do you call a cloud that will never go up because it's lazy?

Fog!

24

What do you call lightning that loves playing sports?

Ball lightning!

25

What would you find cloud wear under its raincoat?

Thunderwear!

26

How do hurricanes see?

With one eye!

27

Where do snowmen keep their money?

In a snow bank.

28

What do you do in the hot weather?

Frying egg whites on the sidewalk.

29

Why shouldn't you complain about the weather?

If it didn't change once in a while, 90% of people would have nothing to talk about.

30

What is electricity?

It is organized lightning.

Chapter 8: Valentine

Even if you aren't into romance, love, or those kissy and mushy blah blahs, you sure love a good joke. Everyone loves jokes. But if you ARE into romance, love, and those kissy and mushy blah blahs like me, then you know Valentine's Day is going to bring us closer to our lovers and expresses the feelings of our hearts.

This is one special day specially created to have some fun, bring a smile to your loved one's face, and make your love life happier. However, love also hurts because the jokes are funny enough to split your sides. Those are the two sides of the coin. You cannot have one, you can only have both.

I'd rather make my wife giggle this Valentine's Day with these love-inspired collection of Val's Day jokes. You should do too… to your girlfriend if you aren't married.

1

Why should you not fall in love with a pastry chef?

He will dessert you.

2

What do you call a very small valentine?

A valen-tiny!

3

How did the phone's boyfriend propose to her on Val's Day?

He gave her a ring.

4

What did the boy cat tell the girl cat on Val's Day?

You're simply purrr-fect for me.

5

Where's the best place for hamburgers to take their girlfriend on Val's Day?

To a meat-ball.

6

What is the best candy to give your girlfriend on Val's Day?

Her-She Kisses.

7

Me: **"I love you."**

You: **"Is that you or the wine talking?"**

Me: **"It's me talking to the wine."**

8

What did the man do when he fell in love with his garden?

He wed his plants!

9

Nymphomaniac (nim(p)-fə-ˈmā-nē-yak) n.

Women who are addicted to sex as much as the average man.

10

Why did Cupid make so much money when he went to the casino?

Because he's a Valentine's Card Shark.

11

What did the toast tell the butter on Val's Day?

You'd always be my butter half!

12

What did the first muffin say to the other muffin on Val's Day?

You're my stud-muffin!

13

What did the first watermelon say to the other watermelon on Val's Day?

You're one in a melon!

14

What did the first beet tell the other beet on Valentine's Day?

Seeing you makes my heart beet faster!

15

What happens when you switch to single on Valentine's Day?

You save so much money.

16

What did the first mushroom say to the other mushroom on Val's Day?

"There's so mushroom in my heart for you!"

17

What's the best thing to tell a coffee-lover on Val's Day?

You mean so much to me words cannot espresso it.

18

Why did my girlfriend give me a cannoli for Val's Day?

Because I told her I cannoli be happy when I'm with her.

19

What's the difference between a $20 steak and a $55 steak?

February 14th.

20

Do you have a date for Valentine's day?

Yes, February 14th.

21

What is the difference between a sailor who falls into the ocean and a girl who is tired of her boyfriend?

One is man overboard and the other is bored over man.

22

Why is lettuce the most loving vegetable?

Because it's all heart.

23

What did the rabbit say to her boyfriend on Valentine's Day?

Somebunny loves you!

24

What did the whale's girlfriend ask him on Valentine's Day?

Whale you keep being mine?

25

What did the male bear tell the female bear on Valentine's Day?

I love you beary much!

26

What did the queen bee say to the king bee on Valentine's Day?

You are so bee-utiful!

27

What did the boy sheep tell the girl sheep on Valentine's Day?

You're not looking baaaa-d!

28

What did Frankenstein say to his girlfriend on Valentine's eve?

Will you be my Valenstein!

Chapter 9: Thanksgiving

There once lived a very happy, long-married couple in my area. They loved each other and ran a small farm. However, there was a problem – the husband farts incredibly, and even enjoyed letting out seriously loud ripping farts, especially in bed. His wife complained and pleaded for years in vain. She would normally end her please with, "Mark my words, one day you'll spill your guts out."

Then the eureka moment happened one Thanksgiving morning. While gutting the turkey, she thought to take all the turkey's guts to their bedroom and slip them under her still sleeping husband's cover. And that she did with the intention of teaching him a lesson. She became worried when at 10am the man was yet to come out of the room – shocking for a farmer, she thought. When he finally came down, he was wearing a strange expression and walking even stranger.

He said, "Nancy, you were so right about the farts. I'm ashamed to confess it but it did happen. I farted my guts out, but glory to God and these two fingers, all is well again!"

If you plan to invite guests for a fabulous Thanksgiving feast and you think entertainment will be the only thing missing, look no further. This chapter contains funny Thanksgiving jokes that you can humor your family and friends with. It will keep them laughing throughout dinner and afterwards. Enjoy them below, keep smiling, and give thanks later.

1

After so much eating and playing on Thanksgiving Day, my 3-yer old daughter asked me to carry her. In trying to be mean I asked her if her legs were broken.

She replied, "Yes, they're out of batteries."

2

What would be the result of crossing a ghost with a turkey?

A poultrygeist!

3

Why did the turkey get arrested by the police?

They suspected fowl play.

4

What made the turkey cross the road twice?

He wanted to prove he wasn't a chicken!

5

What happened when the turkey got into trouble?

The stuffing got knocked out of him!

6

What key won't open any door?

A turkey!

7

What did the aunty turkey say to her disobedient nieces and nephew?

If your parents could see you now, they'd turn over in their gravy

8

What's the best weather for a turkey?

Fowl weather!

9

What kind of dance should you do on Thanksgiving?

The turkey trot.

10

What is a small turkey called if a large turkey is called a gobbler?

A Goblet.

11

Who doesn't care about eating at Thanksgiving?

The turkey, because he's already stuffed!

12

Why should the turkey never be set next to the dessert?

Because she will gobble, gobble it up!

13

What is the turkey's phone's ringtone?

Wing, Wing! Wing, Wing!

14

What's the most musical part of a turkey?

The drumstick.

15

What is a turkey's favorite dessert?

Peach gobbler!

16

What sound does a limping turkey make?

Wobble, wobble!

17

What is it called when it rains turkeys?

Fowl weather!

18

What's the secret to an amazing Thanksgiving dinner?

The tur-KEY.

19

Why should a turkey not attend church?

They use fowl language.

20

What do you call it when a turkey fumbles in football?

A fowl play

21

If fruits are gotten from a fruit tree, where are turkeys gotten from?

A poul-tree.

22

Why shouldn't you look at the turkey when he's dressing?

It will make him blush.

23

What makes a turkey, donkey, and monkey similar?

They all have keys.

24

What side of the turkey will you find the most feathers?

The outside!

25

What does a turkey do on a sunny day?

Have a peck-nic!

26

Why do turkeys lay eggs?

Because they would break if they dropped them.

27

What made the turkey refuse dessert?

Because he was stuffed.

Chapter 10: Birthday!

Birthday quotes for me is a bit like prospecting for black gold, even worse. If you don't strike oil for me in two minutes, I get bored. Everyone needs a good birthday joke that can take the cake. There's no need to fake it. Just shake it, bake it, and make it an awesome celebration with funny stuff, like what is in this chapter.

Welcome to the amazing and wonderful world of adulthood! Now come get a job – just read these, memorize, and use at the next birthday.

1

What do you call the love affair between sugar and cream?

The icing on the cake.

2

What speech do you give a friend on her birthday?

Forget about the past, it can't be changed. Forget about the future, it can't be predicted. And forget about the present, I don't have any for you.

3

What kind of birthday did the tree have?

A sappy one!

4

Why is age a relative thing?

Because all your relatives will keep reminding you how old you are.

5

What was the elephant's birthday wish?

A trunk full of gifts.

6

What do you tell your goldfish on her birthday?

Have a fin-tastic day.

7

When does a birthday cake look like a golf ball?

When you slice it.

8

How do you know you are getting old?

When you go to an antique auction and get over three bids on you.

9

Why did the birthday cake go to a psychologist?

It was feeling crumby.

10

Why do teddy bears reject birthday cake when offered?

Because they are stuffed.

11

What type of birthday cake should you get for someone who loves coffee?

Choco-latte.

12

What goes up and never comes down?

Your age.

13

How do statistics relate with birthdays?

It shows that those who have the most birthdays live the longest.

14

Why do you get heartburn every time you eat birthday cake?

Because they don't take off the candle before eating.

15

What do cats eat on their birthdays?

Mice cream and cake.

16

How does Moby Dick celebrate his birthday?

By having a whale of a time.

17

What did the bald guy say for getting a comb as his birthday gift?

Thank you, I'll never part with it.

18

Why do some people hate birthdays?

Because they think too many can kill them.

19

How do pickles celebrate birthdays?

By relishing the moment.

20

What was the pirate's comment on his 80th birthday?

Aye, matey!

21

Where would you find the best birthday gift for a cat?

A cat-alogue.

22

Why do birthday celebrants always feel warm on their birthday?

Because people don't stop toasting them.

23

How does your cake tell you're getting old?

When it has more candles on it than friends at your birthday party.

24

Why is it always a good idea to have babies as friends?

You get free cake once a year for a lifetime.

25

Why do some people never enjoy their surprise birthday parties?

Because all they can think of is how good their friends are at lying to their face.

26

How do you remember birthdays of people you never really know?

Facebook.

27

Why is it good to have birthdays?

Statistics show that people who have more birthdays live the longest!

28

How do you get yourself remembered and cheered up if you feel a bit lonely and forgotten?

Change your birthday on Facebook.

29

What is the best way to remember your wife's birthday?

Forget it once.

30

What is the best way to remember your age?

Don't change it every year.

31

Why should you celebrate birthdays?

You used to be a person trapped in a woman's body. But you were finally born after 9 long months.

32

Who is a person born to be a pessimist?

A person with a B Negative blood type.

33

Why should you congratulate yourself on your birthday?

Because you're still young enough to remember it.

34

What should be your first step when you get a cake as you get older?

Keep a fire extinguisher close to your cake.

Chapter 11: Coffee

I don't know about you, but the first thing I do in the morning is pour myself a nice cup of joe and sit down to draw a list of java jokes. Nothing starts off my day like a hot cup of coffee, well except maybe a list of jokes about the same hot cup of coffee! Decaf, half-caf, half double decaf with a twist of lemon and a pump of pumpkin spice. Name it, I can't keep all these coffee trends straight.

If you're a coffee aficionado, a caffeine addict, or a barista, these are funny jokes about coffee that you'll love. But if you aren't, then get busy brewing a whole pot of decaf! Let others get busy giggling at this list of hilariously caffeinated jokes while drinking their favorite brews which never misses being featured in these monthly coffee subscription boxes.

I'm sure you're awake right now, and in need of an extra kick. And if you're still sleeping, when you wake up, you'll need an extra kick. This collection of coffee jokes will awaken you even if the strongest espresso shot can't.

So, let's wake up and smell the coffee jokes.

1

What happens when you decide to enjoy a hot cup of coffee in the presence of your boss?

He will get you something that will last until the coffee is cold to do.

2

How should you take your coffee?

Very, very seriously.

3

What is Sleep?

A weak substitute for coffee.

4

What is a sad coffee called?

Despresso.

5

What's the best Beatles song?

Latte Be!

6

Why is coffee called mud?

Because it was ground some minutes ago.

7

How are coffee beans and kids alike?

Because they're both always getting grounded!

8

What do we call stealing other people's coffee?

Mugging!

9

How do tech guys drink coffee?

They install Java!

10

What made the hipster burn his tongue?

He drank his coffee before it was cool.

11

What made Italians so good at making coffee?

They know how to espresso themselves.

12

How can a local coffee shop award you "Employee of the Month" when you don't work there?

If you drink too much coffee.

13

What is the most essential meal of the day?

Coffee.

14

When does coffee taste like dirt?

If it was just ground that morning.

15

Where do birds go to get coffee?

The NESTcafe

16

What should be a Korean's soup of the day?

Coffee.

17

What's the opposite of coffee?

Sneezy.

18

What are the two kinds of people we have in this world?

Liars and people who love Starbucks.

19

Why should you not use sugar when you're taking coffee with your partner?

Because you should be sweet enough for each other.

20

What did the barista's Valentine say?

I can't espresso my love for you.

21

How are men and coffee alike?

The best ones are hot and rich and can keep you up all night.

22

How does Moses make his coffee?

He brews.

23

What is the technical term for a cup of coffee at work?

Break fluid

24

What do you call a situation in which you go to a cafe and are sure you've been there before?

Déjà brew

25

What did the Brazilian coffee tell the Indonesian coffee?

"What's Sumatra with you?"

26

What happens when a pair of jumper cables walk into a café?

They begin to look for something to start.

27

Why should you be wary of 5-cent espresso?

It's a cheap shot.

28

Why should you not discuss coffee in polite company?

It could cause a strong and heated debate to start.

29

What do you call a tendency to not start anything until you've had a cup of coffee?

Procaffeinating.

30

What is a yawn?

It is just a silent scream for coffee.

31

Why was the espresso checking his wristwatch?

He was pressed for time.

Chapter 12: General Wordplay

Some people say wordplay jokes are the lowest form of wit. What they don't realize is that they're the favorite form of humor for legends and celebrities like Mark Twain, Oscar Wilde, Dorothy Parker, Benjamin Franklin, and even Shakespeare. How such groan-worthy "art" form can be beloved by such great brains is beyond my comprehension. However, I read a 2016 study by University of Windsor psychologists, which reported that the understanding and appreciation of a punny wordplay joke requires both the left and right sides of your brain working together to discern the meaning of a joke. So, it's safe to say that reading a wordplay joke (even a really, really dumb one) is an exercise for your brain.

Below are some of my favorite wordplay jokes. Show these jokes some respect, because they are probably a little stupid and silly to you. They'll take both hemispheres of your brain to make sense of them.

1

What is brown and sounds like a bell?

Dung!

2

Why do cannibals not eat comedians?

'cos they taste funny.

3

What made the banker leave his girlfriend?

He lost interest.

4

Why couldn't the Indian get into the hotel?

He didn't have a reservation.

5

Why made Mozart not find his teacher?

Because he was Haydn.

6

Hello, this vacuum cleaner cuts your work in half.

Fantastic, I'll buy two.

7

Mrs. Johnson, I have terrible news. You have cancer and Alzheimer's.

Oh, at least I don't have cancer.

8

What's green and hangs from trees?

Giraffe snot

9

Why can lawyers never be eaten by sharks?

Professional courtesy.

10

What is an aardvark that has been beaten up called?

A vark.

11

Why is a doctor different from God?

God doesn't think he is a doctor!

12

What made the whale jump out of the water?

He wanted to get to the other side.

13

What did the policeman do when he found three men in bed with his wife?

'Ello. 'Ello. 'Ello!

14

How can a handkerchief dance be made?

Put a little boogey in it.

15

How can an elephant be hidden in a cherry tree?

Paint its toenails red!

16

What do you read white and black all over?

A used newspaper!

17

Did you hear about the wedding of the two antennae?

It wasn't really good, but the reception was amazing!

18

Did you hear about the scarecrow that won a Nobel prize?

He was said to be out, standing in his field.

19

What is a woman with one shorter leg called?

Ilene

20

What is she called if she's Japanese?

Irene

21

What is the result of crossing a kangaroo with an elephant?

Big holes everywhere in Australia!!

22

Who won the boxing match between the hedgehog and the beaver?

The hedgehog, on points.

23

What is white, blue and green?

A fridge wearing jeans sitting in a field!!!

24

What is an Italian with a rubber toe called?

Roberto

25

Two cows were discussing in a field.

The first cow said, "Moo," the second cow replied, "You spoke my heart!"

26

What's Brown, sits on a tree, yet can't sing?

Des O' Conker

27

How can a circus be killed?

Go for the juggler.

28

How can a duck be turned into a soul singer?

Shove it in the oven and wait till its Bill Withers.

29

Why was the Swedish factory worker sacked?

Because he never stopped taking stock home! (stockholm!)

30

What happened when Shakespeare walked into a pub?

The blonde at the counter said, "I am not serving you mate, you're Bard."

31

What did the first parrot sitting on the perch say to the other?

Can you smell fish?

32

What is red and invisible?

No tomatoes.

33

Homer, you don't listen to anything I say!

Thanks, I would love an omlet.

34

What is a mushroom who buys everyone drinks all night called?

A real Fungi to be with.

35

How do you compliment a fast driver?

Leave a note on his windscreen saying parking fine.

36

What made the egg cross the road?

It wants to research its genealogy.

37

What was the monk's conclusion upon returning to his monastery after traveling round the world?

The world is my cloister.

38

What is black, shiny, and sails the seven seas?

Binbag the sailor!

39

What is more courageous, a rock or a stump?

A rock, because it's more boulder.

40

How much was the neutron charged for the drink he bought from the bar?

No charge.

41

Where are the armies of a King kept?

In his sleevies.

42

Where do we call the places horses go when they are hurt or injured?

The Horsepital.

43

What made the mouse squeak?

It needed oiling

44

What is produced from the cross between a rhino and an elephant?

Hellifino.

45

Name 2 crustaceans

King Crustacean & Charring Crustacean

46

Why can't a mouse be milked?

'cos it's not possible to get a bucket under it

47

What is red and sits in one corner?

A naughty bus!

48

Why did the chicken cross the road?

To meet the rooster on the other side of the road.

49

How can a running nose be stopped from running?

Teach it to WALK!

50

What food can you buy at the Cyber Cafe?

Micro Chips

51

What was born to succeed?

A budgie with a blunt beak!

52

Why does a gorilla have big nostrils?

Because its fingers are big!

53

How much is a pirate charged to pierce his ear?

A Buccaner (buck an ear)

54

Windows Operating System

The world's best World's best oxymoron

55

Did you hear what happened to the hyena who swallowed an Oxo cube?

He became a laughing stock.

56

The doctor told her to take one pill per day for the rest of her life. Guess what?

He gave her 4 pills.

57

What happened to the Invisible Man that got married to the Invisible Woman?

Their kids aren't exactly much to look at.

58

How can an idiot be kept in suspense?

I will tell you later

59

What always makes one side of a "V" of geese longer?

'cos more geese are on that side.

60

What happened to the magic tractor?

It was going down the road and turned into a field.

61

Why do cannibals hate clowns?

Because they taste funny!

62

Why do cannibals love missionaries?

Because they get to taste Christianity!

63

What is a musician whose girlfriend has dumped him called?

Homeless.

64

What is red but stands in the corner?

A naughty strawberry

65

What do you use a wombat for?

To play Wom.

66

How is a bison different from a buffalo?

You can't wash in a buffalo

67

Who is the penguin's best relative?

Her Aunt Artica!

68

Why did we have a fish in the piano?

It was a piano tuna

69

What is produced from crossing a dog, a bird, and a car?

A flying carpet

70

What is white but walks through the desert?

A herd of yogurt

71

What differentiates the Prince of Wales from a tennis ball?

One is the heir to a throne and the other is thrown to the air.

72

Why was the fly doing an old-fashioned dance on the jam jar?

Because the cover says "twist to open"

73

What is the result of crossing a vampire with a snowman?

FROSTBITE!!!

74

A square and a circle walk into a bar.

The square tells the circle, "You're round!"

75

What did the policeman tell his belly when he tried looking at it?

You're under a vest!

76

What made the chicken cross the playground?

It wanted to get to the other slide.

77

Why do deep sea divers jump out of the boat backwards when they want to go into the water?

Because they would fall into the boat if they jumped forward.

78

Did you hear about what the mathematician did on Saturday night?

He drank and derived.

79

What did the orange say to the banana on the street corner?

"Hi"

80

Did you hear what Batman told Robin before they entered the car?

Robin, get in the car.

81

How can you catch a rhino wearing a wool-hat?

Kick its back and let it chase you around a lake until it's hot and takes off the hat. Now catch it like you would a normal rhino.

82

What is the best guard for a dog?

The tree, because it has more bark!

83

What's white and black and white and black and white and black?

A penguin rolling down a hill.

84

What's white and black and laughing?

The penguin that pushed the penguin rolling down the hill.

85

What did the small rug say to the large rug?

I'm cold, cover me.

86

How did your telephones get engaged?

They simply gave each other a ring.

87

What do chiropodists have for breakfast?

Cornflakes!

88

What happened to the car mechanic that fell asleep dreaming about cars?

He woke up very exhausted.

89

Why do birds sing, yet humming birds hum?

Humming birds don't usually remember the lyrics.

90

You're an expensive lawyer! Will you answer two questions for me If I give you $500?

Sure! What's your second question?"

91

Michael, why are you late for class?

I was almost at school when I crossed the "SLOW" sign, so I had to go really slow.

92

What's green and sings?

Elvis Parsley.

93

Why do people use the quote, "You never judge someone until you've walked a mile in their shoes?"

Because you'll be a mile away when you do, and still have their shoes.

94

What is produced from crossing a mammal with a reptile?

A Nobel prize.

95

What happens when you don't pay your exorcist?

You get repossessed

96

What has four wheels and flies?

A garbage truck.

97

What differentiates a bagpipe from a trampoline?

You eventually get tired of jumping on a trampoline.

98

Is there something worse than finding a maggot in your orange?

Yes, finding half a maggot in your orange.

99

What do you find at the bottom of the ocean that quivers?

A nervous wreck.

100

What is a princess who worries all the time called?

A warrior princess.

101

What do you call a dog named Minton that ate two shuttlecocks.

Bad Minton!!!!

102

What's white, blue, purple, and black all over?

A zebra with a bruise!

103

That's a really beautiful wig.

How much did you have toupee for it?

104

What is a Swiss Financier on the Paris undergound called?

A metronome.

105

What made the chicken cross the road?

It wanted to show the possum that it could be done.

106

What is a woman who can balance 4 pints of beer on her head called?

Beatrix

107

Why are seagulls called seagulls?

Because they fly over the sea. If they flew over the bay, they'd be bagels.

108

What did the snail do when it rode the turtles back?

It exclaimed WHEEEE!!!

109

What made the teddy bear reject dinner?

It was stuffed.

110

What makes God laugh?

People making plans.

111

Why do elephants drink?

To try and forget

112

What do you call a boomerang that doesn't come back?

A stick.

113

What is a fly without wings called?

A walk.

114

How do Reverend Fathers boil water?

They boil the hell out of it.

115

What did the female volcano ask the male volcano?

Will you lava me as much as I lava you?

116

What happened when the football coach went to the bank?

He got his quarterback!

117

What happened to the ship that ran aground carrying a cargo of black and red paint?

The whole crew got marooned.

118

Why don't clams share their candies?

Because they are shellfish.

119

What is the difference between apathy, ambivalence, and ignorance?

I don't know, I don't care, and I'm not interested whichever way.

Chapter 13: Creative Answering Machine Messages

In 1935, the world's first automated answering machine was invented by Willy Müller. It was a three-foot-tall machine commonly used by Orthodox Jews who don't answer the phone on Sabbath day. In 1960, Dr. Kazuo created the Ansafone, the first answering sold answering machine in the USA. Next, PhoneMate introduced the Model 400 in 1971, one of the first few commercially viable answering machines. It had a weight of 10 pounds and could hold about 20 messages on a reel-to-reel tape.

The story of this invention bores me as much as the standard greeting of, "Hi, this is ____. I'm not here right now. Please leave your message and I'll get back to you" most people have on their voicemails and answering machines.

This chapter contains creative ideas to spice up your answering machine and voicemail greeting with something that will make people think, smile, or laugh. At the end of them, I expect that you should be able to come up with some that resonate with your style.

1

If you are a thief, then we're at home cleaning our weapons at the moment and may not be able to come to the phone. If you aren't a thief, we are probably not at home, it's safe to leave us a message.

2

A is for academics, B is for beer, C is for church. One of those reasons is why we can't reach the phone. So leave us a message.

3

Hi. This is John: If you are my parents, please send some money. If you are a friend, you owe me some money. If you are the bank, you didn't lend me enough money. If you are the phone billing company, I already sent the money. If you are a lady, don't worry, I have plenty of money and I'll be with you soon.

4

Take this story seriously. Mark sits there reading a magazine. All of a sudden, the telephone rang! The toilet exploded into a veritable maelstrom of toilet tissue, with Mark sitting on it, his arms moving back and forth at incredible speeds! Can he make it in time? Alas no, his brave effort is in vain. Now that the bell has sounded, you must leave a message.

5

My husband and I can't come to the phone at the moment, but we'll get back to you once we are done, only if you'll leave your name and number.

6

Hello, you've reached Kim and Kanye. We can't pick up your call right now because we're doing something we really enjoy and aren't in a position to reach the phone. Kim likes doing it left and right, and I like doing it up and down... really slowly. So, please leave a message, and we'll get back to you when we are done brushing our teeth.

7

Hi. Now you say something.

8

Hi, Although I'm not at home at the moment, my answering machine is, and I trust it to speak with you. Wait for the beep." "Hello. I'm Dale's answering machine. What are you?

9

He-lo! This is Sa-to. I call you soon if you leave a message, and I call sooner if you leave a sexy message.

10

Hi! This is Susan's refrigerator, her answering machine broke. Please speak as slowly as you can so that I can use the magnets on me to stick your message to myself.

11

Hello, this is George's microwave. His answering machine just eloped with his tape deck, so I'm stuck with taking his calls until he's back. If you would like to cook anything while recording your message, just hold it up to the phone and trust me.

12

Hi, you are talking to a machine. I have the ability to receive messages. My owners have no need for siding, windows, or a hot tub, and strangely, their carpets are clean. They don't need their picture taken because they give to charity through the office. If you're still there, please leave your number and name and expect them to get back to you.

13

I wish I were just an answering machine, but nah, I am a telepathic thought-recording device. After the beep, think about what I know you as, your reason for trying my line, and a number where I can call you on, and I'll think about getting back to you.

14

Hi. You know, I am probably at home and just avoiding someone I don't exactly like. Please leave a message, but if I don't call back, just know that you're the one.

15

Hi, this is Helen. I'm sorry I can't answer the phone at the moment. Drop a message and wait by your phone until I call you back.

Thank You!

And that's a wrap!

Thanks again for purchasing *"Dad Jokes: The Best Dad Jokes, Awfully Bad but Funny Jokes and Puns Volume 2!"*

I hope you enjoyed and are recovering from these hilarious jokes! If you liked the book, please do write a review on Amazon and tell your friends about this book in case they could use a laugh.

And by the look of some of your friends, I am sure they do!

So, just for you. They say the best way to end a speech is to leave with a bang. I'm ending with a story. I hope it leaves you with a moral… BANG!!!

Tom and Harry went hunting in Minnesota and caught a game. A deer actually. As they dragged their game by the tail to where their truck was, they kept slipping, losing their grip and balance in the process. Suddenly, a farmer came along and asked them, "What are you boys doing?"

"We're dragging the deer to our truck," they replied.

"You shouldn't drag a deer by the tail, it should be dragged at the handles," the farmer said.

"They're called antlers. You should drag it by the antlers," he added.

"Thanks so much for the idea," Tom and Harry said to him

Then they started pulling the deer by the antlers. After about ten minutes of rapid progress, Tom said to Harry, "Harry, the farmer was right about dragging this game by the antlers, it makes it easier."

Harry replied, "Yeah, but aren't we going farther and farther from where the truck is?"

"Most people in life are doing it the easy way, but they are going farther and farther from their goals and objectives."

I got to go, don't be a Tom and Harry, stay focused on cracking ribs, tearing people apart and making everyone happy at the end. This book does the trick.

Don't Forget!

If you don't have an Audible Account and would like to listen to the audio version for FREE…

Click the link below and sign up; to receive **"Dad Jokes: The Best Dad Jokes, Awfully Bad but Funny Jokes and Puns Volume 2"** Audiobook for Free!

For US: http://bit.ly/DadJokes2

For UK: http://bit.ly/DadJokes2UK

www.ingramcontent.com/pod-product-compliance
Lightning Source LLC
Chambersburg PA
CBHW071502080526
44587CB00014B/2189